LE CORDON BLEU

HOME COLLECTION

·PUDDINGS·

MEREHURST

contents

recipe ratings ✦ *easy* ✦✦ *a little more care needed* ✦✦✦ *more care needed*

Chocolate and cardamom brioche-and-butter pudding

A delicious variation on an old favourite, this bread-and-butter pudding is made with rich, yeasty brioche and dark chocolate, and is flavoured with cardamom to give an aromatic twist.

Preparation time **45 minutes + 40 minutes standing**
Total cooking time **50 minutes**
Serves **4–6**

440 ml (14 fl oz) milk
1 vanilla pod, split lengthways
5 cardamoms, lightly crushed
150 g (5 oz) brioche loaf, cut into 1 cm (1/2 inch) slices
30 g (1 oz) unsalted butter, softened
3 eggs
45 g (11/2 oz) caster sugar
100 g (31/4 oz) good-quality dark chocolate,
**   finely chopped**
caster sugar or icing sugar, for dusting

1 Slowly bring the milk, vanilla pod and cardamoms to the boil in a pan. Remove from the stove, then set aside for about 30 minutes for the flavours to infuse. Preheat the oven to warm 160°C (315°F/Gas 2–3) and brush a 23 cm (9 inch) oval pie or ovenproof dish with a little melted butter.

2 Spread one side of each brioche slice with the softened butter. Cut each slice into four triangles and trim off the crusts. Neatly overlap them in the prepared dish, standing the triangles up a little.

3 Whisk the eggs and sugar in a heatproof bowl until pale and thick. Bring the milk back to the boil, then remove from the heat, add the chocolate and stir until the chocolate has melted and the mixture is smooth. Add the chocolate milk to the egg and sugar mixture and stir well, then strain into a jug and discard the cardamoms and vanilla pod.

4 Pour three-quarters of the chocolate liquid onto the brioche until each slice is soaked in the liquid, then stand for 10 minutes for the liquid to soak in. Pour over the remaining chocolate liquid. If you want a crunchier topping, sprinkle the surface of the pudding with a little caster sugar.

5 Place the dish inside a baking dish and pour in enough hot water to come halfway up its sides. Bake for 40–45 minutes, or until the custard is set.

6 Remove from the oven and if you didn't use caster sugar, dust with a little sifted icing sugar. Serve with a spoon of crème fraîche.

Chef's tip For a variation, omit the cardamoms and instead spread a handful of well-drained, canned black cherries evenly over the base of the dish or between the brioche slices.

Traditional Christmas pudding

This richest of fruit puddings surely needs no introduction. This traditional version is easy to make up to a year in advance and can be reheated in just a few hours on Christmas day.

Preparation time **45 minutes + overnight marinating**
Total cooking time **10 hours**
Serves **8**

MARINATED FRUITS
250 g (8 oz) sultanas
250 g (8 oz) raisins
315 g (10 oz) currants
60 g (2 oz) glacé cherries
60 g (2 oz) candied mixed peel
60 g (2 oz) dates, stoned and chopped
1¹/2 teaspoons mixed spice
1 teaspoon ground cinnamon
1 teaspoon ground nutmeg
¹/4 teaspoon ground ginger
grated rind of 2 oranges
juice of 1 orange
grated rind of 1 lemon
105 ml (3¹/2 fl oz) stout
125 ml (4 fl oz) brandy

PUDDING
150 g (5 oz) apples, peeled, cored and
 grated
150 g (5 oz) plain flour
105 g (3¹/2 oz) ground almonds
200 g (6¹/2 oz) suet, grated (see page 63)
150 g (5 oz) dark brown sugar

200 g (6¹/2 oz) fresh white breadcrumbs
2 eggs, beaten
2 tablespoons treacle

3 tablespoons brandy

1 To make the marinated fruits, place all the ingredients into a large bowl and mix together well. Cover with plastic wrap and leave overnight in a cool place.
2 The next day, prepare the pudding by placing all the ingredients into a large bowl and making a well in the centre. Add the marinated fruits and any liquid and mix well to form a soft batter.
3 Prepare one 2.5 litre or two 1.25 litre pudding basins for steaming (see Chef's techniques, page 62). Steam the pudding for 10 hours, following the steaming method in the Chef's techniques on page 62.
4 Allow the pudding to stand for 15 minutes before removing the string, foil and paper and turning out. In a small pan, warm the brandy, then at the table pour it over the pudding and ignite it at arm's length. Serve with the traditional brandy butter or just cream.

Chef's tip To prepare this pudding ahead of time, steam for 8 hours, then leave to cool. Remove the string, foil and paper and check the surface of the pudding is dry. Re-cover with new paper and foil and store somewhere cool until needed. To reheat on the day, steam the pudding for 2 hours, leave for 15 minutes and serve as above.

Fruit cobbler

The name 'cobbler' came from America in the nineteenth century and refers to a fruit pie with a scone topping. This cobbler has a golden hazelnut and apricot topping over summer's late fruit.

*Preparation time **1 hour + 20 minutes refrigeration***
*Total cooking time **40 minutes***

Serves 6

COBBLER TOPPING
310 g (10 oz) plain flour
2 teaspoons baking powder
75 g (2¹/2 oz) unsalted butter, chilled and cut into cubes
45 g (1¹/2 oz) caster sugar
2 eggs, beaten
3 tablespoons milk
100 g (3¹/4 oz) hazelnuts, finely chopped
75 g (2¹/2 oz) dried apricots, finely chopped

FRUIT COMPOTE
55 g (1³/4 oz) caster sugar
25 g (³/4 oz) unsalted butter
2 cloves
1 cinnamon stick
¹/2 vanilla pod, split lengthways
2 dessert apples, peeled, cored and cut into eighths
2 ripe pears, peeled, cored and chopped into
    2 cm (³/4 inch) pieces
3 fresh apricots, halved and stoned,
    or 6 canned apricot halves
2 fresh peaches, halved, stoned and cut into eighths,
    or 4 canned peach halves, sliced
3 fresh plums, halved and stoned, or
    3 canned and stoned dark plums, halved
finely grated rind of 1 lemon
finely grated rind of ¹/2 orange
pinch of ground mixed spice
pinch of ground cinnamon

1 egg yolk
icing sugar, for dusting

1   Brush a round 21 cm (8¹/2 inch) diameter and 4 cm (1¹/2 inch) deep ovenproof dish with melted butter.
2   To make the cobbler topping, sieve the flour and baking powder into a bowl. Rub the butter into the flour using your fingertips until the mixture resembles fine breadcrumbs. Lightly stir in the sugar, make a well in the centre and add the eggs and milk. Bring the mixture roughly together using a palette knife. Add the hazelnuts and apricots and bring everything together to form a dough, shape into a ball and flatten slightly. Wrap in plastic wrap and place in the refrigerator for about 20 minutes.
3   To make the fruit compote, first prepare a caramel using the caster sugar and 3 tablespoons water, following the method in the Chef's techniques on page 62. After the caramel has stopped cooking, return to the heat and remelt the caramel gently, then mix in the butter, cloves, cinnamon stick, vanilla and apple and cook, covered, for 5 minutes. Add the pear, apricot, peach and fresh plum, cover and gently cook for about 5 minutes, stirring occasionally. (If using canned plums, add at the end of the 5 minutes cooking time or they will break up.) Discard the flavourings, stir in the lemon and orange rind and the ground spices, and pour the compote into the prepared dish.
4   Preheat the oven to hot 210°C (415°F/Gas 6–7). On a lightly floured surface, roll out the topping dough to 1.5 cm (⁵/8 inch) thick, then cut out circles using a 6 cm (2¹/2 inch) plain cutter. Arrange the circles, slightly overlapping, on top of the hot compote.
5   Beat the egg yolk and 1 teaspoon water together to make an egg wash and brush over the top of the cobbler. Do not brush the cut sides or the egg will set and prevent rising. Bake for 15 minutes, or until well risen and golden brown. Cool for 5–10 minutes before serving, then dust with the sifted icing sugar and serve with cream or ice cream.

Rhubarb crumble

This simple pudding is a great way to use up a glut of ripe, in-season fruit. In this version, tangy rhubarb perfectly complements the buttery, short topping.

Preparation time **30 minutes**
Total cooking time **40 minutes**
Serves 6

2 tablespoons strawberry jam
650 g (1 lb 5 oz) trimmed rhubarb, cut in
 2.5 cm (1 inch) slices
2 tablespoons demerara sugar
60 g (2 oz) wholemeal flour
60 g (2 oz) plain flour
90 g (3 oz) unsalted butter, chilled and cut into cubes
105 g (3¹/2 oz) caster or demerara sugar
1 tablespoon pumpkin seeds, toasted
1 tablespoon hazelnuts, toasted and roughly chopped

1 Place the strawberry jam in a wide, shallow pan with 2 tablespoons water, then add the rhubarb in a single layer with the 2 tablespoons of demerara sugar. Bring to the boil, then immediately lower the heat to a simmer, cover tightly with a lid or piece of foil and cook for about 5 minutes. The acidity of rhubarb does vary, so taste and add more sugar if necessary.

2 Transfer the rhubarb into a 1.25 litre ovenproof dish, 20 cm (8 inches) in diameter and 6 cm (2¹/2 inches) deep. Spread out evenly, then pour over enough rhubarb juice to come halfway up the rhubarb. Set aside to cool. Preheat the oven to moderate 180°C (350°F/Gas 4).

3 Sieve the wholemeal and plain flours into a bowl, tipping the bits from the wholemeal flour back into the bowl. Rub the butter into the flour using your fingertips until the mixture resembles fine breadcrumbs. Continue to rub in the butter until small lumps begin to form, then add the sugar, pumpkin seeds and hazelnuts and toss to incorporate.

4 Scatter the crumble mixture evenly over the rhubarb in the dish without pressing it down, then bake for 20–30 minutes, or until the topping is golden brown. Dust with a little extra sugar if you wish, and serve warm or cold with cream.

Eve's pudding

As the name of this English pudding suggests, it should be made with apples, which take on a tempting caramelized sweetness under the light sponge and golden almonds.

Preparation time **25 minutes**
Total cooking time **45 minutes**
Serves 6

APPLE COMPOTE
55 g (1³/4 oz) unsalted butter, softened
75 g (2¹/2 oz) caster sugar
2 cloves
¹/2 teaspoon ground cinnamon
1 vanilla pod, split lengthways
750 g (1¹/2 lb) Golden Delicious apples, peeled, cored and cut into eighths

ALMOND TOPPING
120 g (4 oz) unsalted butter, at room temperature
120 g (4 oz) caster sugar
finely grated rind of 1 lemon
¹/2 teaspoon vanilla extract or essence
3 eggs, beaten
25 g (³/4 oz) plain flour
120 g (4 oz) ground almonds, sieved
75 g (2¹/2 oz) flaked almonds

2 tablespoons apricot jam
icing sugar, for dusting

1 Brush a 1.5 litre ovenproof dish, 2 cm (³/4 inch) deep, with melted butter.

2 To make the apple compote, place the butter and sugar in a large pan and stir over low heat to melt the butter and dissolve the sugar. Add the cloves, cinnamon and vanilla pod, then add the apple and mix to coat with the butter. Cover and cook very gently for 5 minutes, or until the apple is just starting to soften. Discard the flavourings and spread the mixture evenly over the base of the prepared dish. Set aside to cool. Preheat the oven to moderate 180°C (350°F/Gas 4).

3 To make the almond topping, place the butter, sugar, lemon rind and vanilla in a bowl and, using a wooden spoon or electric beaters, beat until light and creamy. Add the beaten egg in six additions, beating well between each addition. Sieve the flour and a pinch of salt onto the mixture, scatter on the ground almonds and, using a large metal spoon or spatula, fold in gently to combine. Spoon over the apple mixture, smooth the top and sprinkle with the flaked almonds. Bake for about 30–35 minutes, or until the topping is firm to the touch.

4 In a small pan, heat the apricot jam with 2 teaspoons water. When the mixture has melted and begins to boil, sieve it into a small bowl and, while still hot, brush it over the surface of the pudding. Leave for 1 minute, then dust with the sifted icing sugar. Serve with cream.

Ginger pudding with kumquat and ginger compote

*This warming winter pudding is made with treacle, syrup and ginger and is
a perfect match for the tart kumquat and ginger compote.*

Preparation time *1 hour 30 minutes + overnight standing*
Total cooking time *2 hours 30 minutes*
Serves 6

GINGER AND KUMQUAT COMPOTE
675 g (1 lb 6 oz) ripe kumquats, quartered and seeded
500 g (1 lb) caster sugar
50 g (1³/4 oz) preserved stem ginger, chopped
  (drained weight, reserving 120 ml/4 fl oz syrup)

GINGER PUDDING
125 g (4 oz) preserved stem ginger
  (drained weight, reserving 1 tablespoon syrup)
1 tablespoon golden syrup
120 g (4 oz) unsalted butter, at room temperature
90 g (3 oz) soft light brown sugar
30 g (1 oz) treacle
3 eggs, beaten
180 g (5³/4 oz) self-raising flour
1 teaspoon ground ginger
2 tablespoons milk

1 To make the ginger and kumquat compote, place the kumquats, sugar and ginger in a bowl and stir to combine. Cover and stand overnight in a cool place to allow the sugar to dissolve and the juice to start running from the fruit.

2 Tip the fruit and sugary juices into a large pan and add the ginger syrup and 500 ml (16 fl oz) water. Slowly bring to the boil over low heat, stirring until any remaining sugar has dissolved. Skim off any surface foam with a metal spoon. Raise the heat and boil hard, without stirring, for 15–20 minutes, or until the compote has thickened and is slightly syrupy. Remove from the heat and allow to cool.

3 To make the ginger pudding, prepare a 1.25 litre pudding basin for steaming (see Chef's techniques, page 62).

4 Slice 75 g (2¹/2 oz) of the ginger thinly, then finely dice the remainder. Using the ginger slices, arrange a five-petal flower in the bottom of the pudding basin, then continue to form flower patterns up the sides of the basin until they reach two-thirds of the way up.

5 In a small pan, gently warm the golden syrup so it flows easily, then pour it into the bottom of the basin without dislodging the ginger flowers.

6 Place the butter and sugar in a bowl and, using a wooden spoon or electric beaters, beat together until light and creamy, then stir in the treacle and reserved ginger syrup. Add the beaten egg in six additions, beating well between each addition. Sieve the flour, ground ginger and a pinch of salt onto the mixture and fold in using a large metal spoon or plastic spatula, then briskly fold in the milk and finely diced ginger.

7 Spoon the mixture into the prepared pudding basin, cover and steam for 2 hours, following the steaming method in the Chef's techniques on page 62. To test when the pudding is done, pierce with a skewer. If it comes out clean, the pudding is cooked. Remove the string, foil and paper and turn out. Serve with the compote and some lightly whipped cream.

Chef's tip To store excess compote, sterilize some jars and lids by washing them in hot soapy water. Rinse out, then dry in a very slow 120°C (250°F/Gas 1–2) oven for 20 minutes. Pour in the compote, seal the jars, date and store somewhere cool. Use as a sauce for ice cream.

Schmarrn

Kaiserschmarrn is a deliciously simple Austrian pudding of fried crêpes, often served with a fruit compote. This variation includes the crêpes, a fruity plum marmalade and smooth custard all in one dish.

Preparation time **1 hour + 30 minutes refrigeration**
   + 15 minutes cooling
Total cooking time **1 hour 45 minutes**
Serves **6**

CREPES
75 g (2¹/₂ oz) plain flour
I tablespoon caster sugar
I egg
¹/₄ teaspoon vanilla extract or essence
200 ml (6¹/₂ fl oz) milk

clarified butter or oil, for frying
3 tablespoons apricot jam
30 g (I oz) toasted flaked almonds
icing sugar, for dusting

PLUM MARMALADE
345 g (I I oz) fresh red plums, stoned and roughly
   chopped or 825 g (I lb I I oz) canned plums,
   drained, stoned and roughly chopped
45–90 g (I¹/₂–3 oz) caster sugar
I cinnamon stick
¹/₂ vanilla pod, split lengthways

CUSTARD
185 ml (6 fl oz) milk
185 ml (6 fl oz) cream
I vanilla pod, split lengthways
3 eggs
I egg yolk
75 g (2¹/₂ oz) caster sugar

1 To make the crêpes, sieve the flour into a bowl with the sugar and a small pinch of salt. Make a well in the centre, add the egg and vanilla and begin to whisk in the flour. As it starts to thicken, add the milk gradually until all the flour is incorporated and the batter is smooth and lump-free. Cover and refrigerate for 30 minutes.

2 Cook the crêpes following the method in the Chef's techniques on page 63, turning out finished ones onto a sheet of greaseproof paper and covering with a tea towel.

3 To make the plum marmalade, place the plums, sugar (the plums will need less sugar if they are very ripe), cinnamon stick and vanilla in a pan and cook, covered, over low heat for 15 minutes, or until the mixture is soft and very thick. If there is too much juice, remove the lid and cook, uncovered, until the plums have a sticky, jam-like consistency. Set aside to cool for 15 minutes, then remove the cinnamon and vanilla pod.

4 Spread the plum marmalade over the crêpes and roll up tightly to form long cigar shapes. Slice into 1 cm (¹/₂ inch) pieces. Brush a shallow 1-litre ovenproof dish with butter, then arrange the slices in it, cut-side-up. Preheat the oven to moderate 180°C (350°F/Gas 4).

5 To make the custard, place the milk, cream and vanilla pod in a pan and bring slowly to the boil. Remove from the heat. In a bowl, using a wooden spoon or electric beaters, cream together the eggs, yolk and sugar until pale and thick. Pour the hot milk onto the eggs and mix well, then discard the pod and strain into a jug.

6 Pour the custard over the crêpes and place the dish inside a baking dish. Pour in enough hot water to come halfway up its sides. Bake for 40 minutes, or until the top is firm to the touch.

7 In a small pan, heat the apricot jam with 1 tablespoon water. When the mixture has melted and begins to boil, sieve it into a small bowl and, while still hot, brush it over the surface of the pudding. Leave to cool, then decorate with the almonds and sifted icing sugar. Serve with cream.

Queen of puddings

A classic English pudding that dates back to the nineteenth century, the Queen of puddings is created from layers of smooth custard, soft red fruit and jam, topped with a crisp crown of meringue.

*Preparation time **25 minutes***
*Total cooking time **35 minutes***
*Serves **6***

FRUIT PUREE
400 g (12³/4 oz) raspberries or strawberries
lemon juice, to taste
icing sugar, to taste

85 g (2³/4 oz) unsalted butter
150 g (5 oz) fresh bread or cake crumbs
160 g (5¹/4 oz) caster sugar
finely grated rind of 1 lemon
6 egg yolks
95 g (3¹/4 oz) fresh raspberries
95 g (3¹/4 oz) fresh strawberries, quartered
95 g (3¹/4 oz) fresh blueberries
95 g (3¹/4 oz) raspberry jam
4 egg whites
icing sugar, for dusting

1 Preheat the oven to moderate 180°C (350°F/Gas 4). Brush a shallow 25 x 18 cm (10 x 7 inch) ovenproof dish with melted butter.

2 To make the fruit purée, place the raspberries or strawberries in a blender or food processor and process. Add lemon juice and icing sugar to taste, depending on the ripeness of the fruit, then pass the purée through a fine sieve.

3 In a small pan, melt the butter, then remove from the heat. Place the crumbs, 2 tablespoons of the caster sugar and the lemon rind in a bowl and combine. Make a well in the centre and pour in the fruit purée, melted butter and the egg yolks and beat to form a smooth paste.

4 Arrange the raspberries, strawberries and blueberries in the prepared dish and pour the egg mixture over the fruit. Bake for 25 minutes, or until set. Remove from the oven and allow to cool a little. Raise the oven temperature to moderately hot 200°C (400°F/Gas 6).

5 Soften the raspberry jam by beating it in a small bowl with a wooden spoon, then gently spread over the cooked fruit and custard base in the dish.

6 Place the egg whites in a clean dry bowl and beat with a balloon whisk or electric beaters until soft peaks form. Gradually add the remaining caster sugar, beating well between each addition, until stiff glossy peaks form. Spoon into a piping bag with a large star nozzle.

7 Pipe the meringue around the edge of the dish. Dust with sifted icing sugar and bake for 3–5 minutes, or until the meringue is golden brown and crisp. Serve warm or cold with cream.

Lemon and lavender rice soufflés

These light soufflé puddings combine the freshness of lemon with the gentle aroma of lavender.

Preparation time **15 minutes + cooling**
Total cooking time **1 hour 15 minutes**
Serves 6–8

75 g (2 1/2 oz) long-grain rice
750 ml (24 fl oz) milk
finely grated rind of 1 lemon
1/2 teaspoon dried lavender, finely chopped
1/2 vanilla pod, split lengthways
1 egg white
45 g (1 1/2 oz) caster sugar

1 Place the rice in a sieve and rinse thoroughly under running water until the water runs clear, then drain.
2 Pour the milk into a heavy-based pan, add the lemon rind, lavender, vanilla pod and rice and slowly bring to the boil. Reduce the heat and simmer, stirring often, for 40 minutes, or until the mixture is soft and creamy and when a spoon is drawn across the base of the pan, a soft parting line is left behind. Set aside to cool completely.
3 Preheat the oven to moderate 180°C (350°F/Gas 4). Lightly brush eight 8 x 4 cm (3 x 1 1/2 inch) ramekins or an oval 24 x 4 cm (9 1/2 x 1 1/2 inch) ovenproof dish with melted butter.
4 Place the egg white in a clean dry bowl and beat with a balloon whisk or electric beaters until soft peaks form. Add half the sugar and beat until stiff glossy peaks form. Sprinkle on the remaining sugar and, using a plastic spatula or a large metal spoon, gently fold in to form meringue. Check that the rice is still creamy (add a tablespoon of cold milk if necessary), then remove the vanilla pod and fold in the meringue.
5 Three-quarter fill the prepared dishes, place on a baking tray and bake for 20–25 minutes, or until well risen and golden brown. Serve with berries and cream.

Spotted dick

The origin of the name of this classic English suet and raisin pudding is not known, though it seems that dick may have been a general nineteenth century term for pudding. Spotted dick is sometimes known by the equally unusual name of Spotted dog.

Preparation time **15 minutes + 1 hour soaking**
Total cooking time **2 hours**
Serves 6–8

105 g (3¹/₂ oz) currants
135 g (4¹/₂ oz) raisins
2 tablespoons brandy
240 g (7¹/₂ oz) self-raising flour
120 g (4 oz) grated suet (see page 63)
grated rind of 1 lemon
pinch of grated nutmeg
45 g (1¹/₂ oz) caster sugar
150 ml (5 fl oz) milk

1 Place the currants, raisins and brandy in a bowl, cover with plastic wrap and set aside for at least 1 hour, or overnight, to soak.

2 Sieve the flour and a pinch of salt into a bowl and stir in the suet, lemon rind, nutmeg and sugar. Add the soaked fruit and brandy, then the milk, and mix with a wooden spoon to form a firm dough.

3 Lay a sheet of greaseproof paper on a work surface and form the mixture into a roll shape, 20 cm (8 inches) long. Roll the pudding in the paper and fold up the ends, taking care not to wrap it too tightly as the pudding will expand as it cooks.

4 Wrap the roll in a tea towel, put in the top of a bamboo or metal steamer, cover and steam for 2 hours. Do not let the pudding boil dry—replenish with boiling water as it cooks. Unroll from the paper, cut into slices and serve with custard.

Chef's tip If your steamer will not fit a 20 cm (8 inch) pudding, make the pudding shorter and fatter and cook for 15–20 minutes longer.

Rum babas

Spongy yeast cakes soaked in a rum syrup, which are said to have been named by a Polish king after his storybook hero, Ali Baba. Here they are served with a vanilla-flavoured Chantilly cream and fresh fruit.

Preparation time **1 hour + 1 hour proving**
Total cooking time **30 minutes**
Serves **8**

BABA DOUGH
250 g (8 oz) plain or bread flour
1 teaspoon salt
1 teaspoon caster sugar
15 g (1/2 oz) fresh yeast or 7 g (1/4 oz) dry yeast
80 ml (2³/4 fl oz) milk
3 eggs, beaten
60 g (2 oz) raisins, soaked in 1 tablespoon rum
45 g (1¹/2 oz) melted butter, just warm

SYRUP
500 ml (16 fl oz) water
200 g (6¹/2 oz) caster sugar
rind of 1 lemon
1 cardamom pod
2 bay leaves
1/2 orange, roughly chopped
2 tablespoons dark rum

CHANTILLY CREAM
315 g (10 oz) thick (double) cream
30 g (1 oz) icing sugar
1/2 teaspoon vanilla extract or essence

3 tablespoons apricot jam
fresh fruit, such as strawberries and raspberries,
   to decorate

1 Brush eight individual dariole moulds or a 1-litre capacity ring mould with melted butter, then dust with some flour and tap out the excess.

2 To make the baba dough, sieve the flour, salt and sugar into a large bowl and make a well in the centre. Place the yeast in a bowl. In a small pan, warm the milk until tepid, then add to the yeast. Stir to dissolve, then mix in 1 tablespoon flour and set aside until foamy. When foamy, add to the beaten eggs and pour into the well in the flour. Prepare the baba dough following the method in the Chef's techniques on page 63. Preheat the oven to hot 210°C (415°F/Gas 6–7).

3 Bake the rum babas for 12 minutes (25 minutes for a large one), or until golden. Loosen the babas and turn out of the tins onto a wire rack to cool. Prick all over with a fine skewer.

4 To make the syrup, gently heat all the ingredients except the rum together in a pan, stirring to dissolve the sugar, then bring to the boil and boil for 15 minutes to reduce the syrup and thicken slightly. Remove the pan from the stove and leave for 5 minutes to infuse the flavours. Strain, discard the flavourings, return the syrup to the pan and reheat. Remove from the stove and stir in the rum. Pour the syrup into a shallow dish and roll the cold babas in the hot syrup. Place on a wire rack over a plate to drip off excess syrup and to cool completely.

5 To make the Chantilly cream, pour the cream into a bowl and add the icing sugar and vanilla. Using a balloon whisk or electric beaters, whip the cream until it just forms soft peaks that hold as the whisk is lifted from the bowl.

6 In a small pan, heat the apricot jam with 1 tablespoon water. When the mixture has melted and begins to boil, sieve it into a small bowl and, while still hot, brush it over the babas, then leave to cool.

7 Serve the babas with the Chantilly cream and fruit. If you made a large one, fill it with the cream and fruit.

Layered blackcurrant pudding

This sharp but fruity blackcurrant pudding can be made with fresh or frozen berries.

Preparation time **35 minutes**
Total cooking time **2 hours**
Serves 6

180 g (5³/4 oz) unsalted butter, at room temperature
180 g (5³/4 oz) caster sugar
grated rind of 1 lemon
3 eggs, beaten
180 g (5³/4 oz) self-raising flour
3 tablespoons milk
4 tablespoons blackcurrant jam, beaten until smooth
50 g (1³/4 oz) frozen blackcurrants, thawed,
  or topped and tailed fresh blackcurrants

1 Prepare a 1.25 litre pudding basin for steaming (see Chef's techniques, page 62).

2 Place the butter and sugar in a bowl and, using a wooden spoon or electric beaters, beat together until light and creamy. Add the rind, then the beaten egg in six additions, beating well between each addition. Sieve the flour and a pinch of salt onto the mixture and fold in using a large metal spoon or plastic spatula, then briskly fold in the milk.

3 Place a tablespoon of jam in the base of the prepared basin and arrange the blackcurrants on top. Spread a quarter of the sponge mixture over the fruit, followed by a tablespoon of the jam. Continue layering, with the final layer being the remaining sponge mixture. Cover and steam for 2 hours, following the steaming method in the Chef's techniques on page 62. To test when the pudding is done, pierce with a skewer. If it comes out clean, the pudding is cooked.

4 Allow the pudding to stand for 15 minutes before removing the string, foil and paper and turning out.

Pear flapjack pudding

This pudding is a great way to use ripe pears when in season, with a perfect combination of warm cinnamon-pear filling and a crunchy flapjack topping.

*Preparation time **30 minutes***
*Total cooking time **1 hour 45 minutes***
Serves 4–6

PEAR FILLING
60 g (2 oz) unsalted butter
125 g (4 oz) demerara sugar
finely grated rind of 1 orange
finely grated rind of 1 lemon
1/2 teaspoon cinnamon
6 ripe pears (about 1 kg/2 lb in total), peeled, cored and cut into 1 cm (1/2 inch) cubes

FLAPJACK
75 g (2 1/2 oz) unsalted butter
60 g (2 oz) caster sugar
2 tablespoons golden syrup
155 g (5 oz) rolled oats
90 g (3 oz) skinned hazelnuts, roasted and roughly crushed
125 g (4 oz) self-raising flour
1 egg, beaten

1 tablespoon caster sugar
1/2 teaspoon ground cinnamon

1 To make the pear filling, place the butter, demerara sugar, orange and lemon rind and the cinnamon in a pan and heat gently for about 5 minutes, stirring to dissolve the sugar. Increase the heat to medium and cook for another 5 minutes, or until the mixture bubbles and looks golden. Add the pear and cook gently for about 8–10 minutes, or until the pieces are just tender to the point of a sharp knife. Remove from the stove and leave the pears to cool in the pan.

2 To make the flapjack mixture, place the butter, sugar, golden syrup and 2 teaspoons water in a pan and heat gently, stirring until smooth. Bring to the boil, then remove from the stove and stir in the rolled oats, hazelnuts, flour and egg.

3 Spoon a third of the flapjack mixture into the base of a 16 x 6 cm (6 1/2 x 2 1/2 inch) heatproof round dish. Use the back of a spoon to flatten and press the mixture against the base and a little way up the sides, to a thickness of 1 cm (1/2 inch). Using a slotted spoon, lift the pear pieces from the pan and into the dish, then add 4 tablespoons of juice from the pan. Spoon the remaining flapjack mixture on top of the pear and spread evenly to cover, then lightly smooth the top using the back of the spoon. Cover with foil and seal well around the edge of the dish by tying a piece of string around the foil.

4 Place a saucer or trivet in a large pan and rest the dish on it. Pour in boiling water to come halfway up the dish and bring to the boil. Cover and steam the pudding for 1 hour 20 minutes, or until the topping feels firm when pressed, topping up the water if needed with more boiling water.

5 Remove the dish from the water and wipe it dry. Mix together the sugar and cinnamon and dust over the top. Serve with ice cream or crème anglaise (see page 43).

Chocolate-chip pudding with chocolate sauce

This recipe provides a double-chocolate hit, with a rich hot or cold chocolate sauce to pour over a chocolate-chip pudding. Alternatively, you could serve the pudding with just cream or crème anglaise.

*Preparation time **45 minutes***
*Total cooking time **2 hours 15 minutes***
Serves 6

120 g (4 oz) unsalted butter, at room temperature
120 g (4 oz) light soft brown sugar
1 teaspoon vanilla extract or essence
4 eggs, beaten
120 g (4 oz) self-raising flour
30 g (1 oz) cocoa powder
1 tablespoon milk
30 g (1 oz) dark chocolate chips or drops
50 g (1³/4 oz) white chocolate chips or drops

CHOCOLATE SAUCE
225 g (7¹/4 oz) caster sugar
100 g (3¹/4 oz) good-quality dark chocolate, chopped
2 tablespoons cocoa powder, sifted

1 Prepare a 1.25 litre pudding basin for steaming (see Chef's techniques, page 62).

2 Place the butter and sugar in a bowl and, using a wooden spoon or electric beaters, beat together until light and creamy, then mix in the vanilla. Add the beaten egg in six additions, beating well between each addition. Sieve the flour, cocoa powder and a pinch of salt onto the mixture and fold in using a large metal spoon or plastic spatula, then briskly fold in the milk and both the dark and white chocolate chips.

3 Spoon the mixture into the prepared pudding basin, cover and steam for 2 hours, following the steaming method in the Chef's techniques on page 62. To test when the pudding is done, pierce with a skewer. If it comes out clean, the pudding is cooked.

4 To make the chocolate sauce, place 300 ml (10 fl oz) water into a pan with the sugar and chocolate. Bring to the boil slowly, stirring continuously to dissolve the sugar, then remove from the heat. Mix the cocoa with 30 ml (1 fl oz) water to form a smooth paste, add to the pan, stir and return to medium heat. Bring back to the boil, whisking vigorously, then simmer for 5 minutes without allowing the sauce to boil. Strain through a fine sieve and leave to cool a little. The chocolate sauce can be served warm or cold.

5 Remove the string, foil and paper from the pudding and allow to stand for 5–10 minutes before turning out. Serve with the chocolate sauce.

Chef's tip For a more chocolate-flavoured pudding, replace the white chocolate chips with dark chips.

Treacle pudding

This family favourite is rich with golden syrup and is served with a delicious cinnamon-flavoured syrup that should be poured over just before serving.

*Preparation time **35 minutes***
*Total cooking time **2 hours***
*Serves **6***

240 g (7¹/₂ oz) unsalted butter, at room temperature
240 g (7¹/₂ oz) caster sugar
4 eggs, beaten
¹/₂ teaspoon vanilla extract or essence
finely grated rind of 2 lemons
240 g (7¹/₂ oz) self-raising flour
120 g (4 oz) golden syrup

GOLDEN SYRUP SAUCE
1 cinnamon stick
¹/₄ vanilla pod
150 g (5 oz) golden syrup
grated rind and juice of 1 lemon

1 Prepare a 2 litre pudding basin for steaming (see Chef's techniques, page 62).

2 Place the butter and sugar in a bowl and, using a wooden spoon or electric beaters, beat together until light and creamy. Add the beaten egg in six additions, beating well between each addition, then mix in the vanilla and lemon rind. Sieve the flour onto the mixture and fold in using a large metal spoon or plastic spatula.

3 Place the golden syrup in the base of the pudding basin and spoon the sponge mixture on top. Cover and steam for 1 hour 40 minutes, following the steaming method in the Chef's techniques on page 62. To test when the pudding is done, pierce with a skewer. If it comes out clean, the pudding is cooked (though it may still look a bit sticky from the syrup).

4 To make the golden syrup sauce, place the cinnamon, vanilla, golden syrup, lemon juice and rind and 300 ml (10 fl oz) water into a pan and bring to the boil. Simmer for about 15 minutes to reduce by one-third, then remove and discard the cinnamon stick and vanilla pod.

5 Allow the pudding to stand for 10 minutes before removing the string, foil and paper. Serve with the golden syrup sauce.

Sticky toffee puddings

These puddings are also known as sticky date puddings, as dates are the secret ingredient that make the puddings so delicious, while the toffee sauce ensures they remain famously sticky.

Preparation time **40 minutes + 1 hour soaking**
Total cooking time **40 minutes**
Serves **10**

200 g (6¹/2 oz) dates, pitted and chopped
45 g (1¹/2 oz) raisins
grated rind of ¹/2 lemon
1 teaspoon bicarbonate of soda
2 tablespoons coffee essence or 1 tablespoon instant
  coffee mixed with 2 tablespoons boiling water
115 g (3³/4 oz) unsalted butter, at room temperature
180 g (5³/4 oz) soft light brown sugar
4 eggs, beaten
240 g (7¹/2 oz) self-raising flour

TOFFEE SAUCE
1 vanilla pod, split lengthways
60 g (2 oz) unsalted butter
150 g (5 oz) demerara sugar
150 ml (5 fl oz) thick (double) cream

1 Brush ten 175 ml (5³/4 fl oz) pudding moulds or ramekins with melted butter and chill before brushing again, then dust with flour and tap out the excess. Preheat the oven to moderate 180°C (350°F/Gas 4).
2 Place the dates, raisins and lemon rind in a bowl. Sprinkle over the bicarbonate of soda and coffee essence, pour on 300 ml (10 fl oz) boiling water, cover and set aside to soak for one hour.
3 Place the butter and sugar in a bowl and, using a wooden spoon or electric beaters, beat until light and creamy. Add the beaten eggs in six additions, beating well between each addition. Sieve the flour and a pinch of salt onto the mixture and fold in using a large metal spoon or plastic spatula. Add the date and raisin mixture with its liquid and stir gently to make a loose batter.
4 Spoon the mixture into the moulds to three-quarters full. Make a slight hollow in the centre of the mixture and bake for about 20–30 minutes, or until springy to the touch.
5 To make the toffee sauce, scrape the vanilla seeds into the pan and add the pod, butter, sugar and cream and stir for about 3 minutes to dissolve the sugar, then simmer over low-medium heat, without stirring, until smooth and golden brown. Remove and discard the vanilla pod, set the sauce aside and keep warm.
6 When the puddings are cooked, allow to stand for 10 minutes, then turn out. Serve warm with the toffee sauce and whipped cream.

Chef's tip If 10 puddings are too many, you could either halve the recipe or freeze the extra puddings. When you are ready to use the frozen puddings, defrost, then wrap in foil and reheat in a moderate 180°C (350°F/Gas 4) oven for about 20 minutes.

Summer puddings

Perfect for entertaining, these pretty puddings need to be prepared the day before to allow the fruit juices to flavour the bread and turn it that distinctive vivid pink colour.

*Preparation time **30 minutes + overnight refrigeration***
*Total cooking time **5 minutes***
Serves 6

18 thin slices good-quality 1-day-old white bread
1 kg (2 lb) mixed soft fruits, such as blackberries,
**   raspberries, strawberries and blackcurrants,**
**   fresh or frozen and hulled**
90 g (3 oz) caster sugar, depending on the sweetness
**   of the fruit**

1 Cut the crusts from the bread and discard. Reserving two or three slices for the top, cut circles and strips out of the remaining slices to line the base and sides of six 155 ml (5 fl oz) ramekins or pudding moulds, or a 1 litre pudding basin. Make sure the ramekins or basin are completely lined and that there are no spaces between the slices of bread.

2 Halve or quarter the strawberries if large, then place all the fruit in a large pan with 2 tablespoons water and the sugar, to taste. Cover and cook over low heat for about 5 minutes, or until the juices are running from the fruit and they are just tender but still whole.

3 Ladle the fruit and juices into the bread-lined ramekins or basin until it reaches almost to the top of the bread, reserving any excess. Cover with the reserved slices of bread, trimming to fit snugly onto the surface of the fruit. Place on a tray to catch any excess juices and cover with a plate and a weight of about 1 kg (2 lb) if using the pudding basin, or smaller weights if using the ramekins (you can use cans). Leave overnight on the tray in the refrigerator.

4 When ready to serve, remove the weights and carefully turn out the puddings. Serve cold with the extra fruit and juice spooned over and a sorbet, ice cream or cream.

Chef's tip For the best colour and texture, use fewer strawberries than the other softer and darker fruit.

Pineapple and coconut upside-down pudding

A delicious variation on the traditional pineapple recipe. The caramelized topping that characterizes an upside-down cake is created during baking by the combination of sugar, butter and fruit juices.

Preparation time **30 minutes**
Total cooking time **1 hour 5 minutes**
Serves **6**

100 g (3¹/4 oz) caster sugar
55 g (1³/4 oz) unsalted butter
5–7 canned pineapple rings, well drained
7 glacé cherries, halved

COCONUT SPONGE
150 g (5 oz) unsalted butter, at room temperature
150 g (5 oz) caster sugar
4 eggs
finely grated rind of 1 lemon
180 g (5³/4 oz) plain flour
¹/2 teaspoon baking powder
60 ml (2 fl oz) canned coconut cream
95 g (3¹/4 oz) desiccated coconut

1 Put a 20 x 4 cm (8 x 1¹/2 inch) round sandwich tin onto a sheet of greaseproof paper, trace around the base with a pencil and cut out a circle just inside the pencil marking. Brush the inside of the tin with melted butter and place the paper inside the tin. Preheat the oven to moderate 180°C (350°F/Gas 4).

2 Prepare a caramel using the sugar and 3 tablespoons water, following the method in the Chef's techniques on page 62. After the caramel has stopped cooking, mix in the butter, then reheat the caramel and, when liquid, pour into the prepared tin. Set aside for the caramel to cool. Arrange the pineapple slices on the caramel, trimming them to fit neatly into the tin if necessary, then decorate with the glacé cherries.

3 To make the coconut sponge, place the butter and sugar in a bowl and, using a wooden spoon or electric beaters, beat until light and creamy. Add the beaten egg in six additions, beating well between each addition. Stir in the lemon rind, then sieve the flour and baking powder onto the mixture and beat in with the coconut cream and desiccated coconut until smooth. Immediately spoon on top of the pineapple and make a slight hollow in the centre with the back of a damp spoon.

4 Bake for 1 hour, or until golden. To test when the pudding is done, pierce with a skewer. If it comes out clean, the pudding is cooked. Allow to stand for 5 minutes in the tin, then turn out and serve with cream or crème anglaise (see page 43).

Sussex pond pudding

Inside the light suet pastry is a whole lemon, sugar and butter which, when the pudding is cut into, causes a flood of lemony juices to rush out to form a pond of sauce.

*Preparation time **30 minutes + 20 minutes standing***
*Total cooking time **3 hours***
*Serves **4–6***

FILLING
240 g (7¹/₂ oz) unsalted butter, softened
120 g (4 oz) light soft brown sugar
120 g (4 oz) demerara sugar
1 thin-skinned lemon, washed

SUET CRUST
180 g (5³/₄ oz) self-raising flour
grated rind of 1 lemon
75 g (2¹/₂ oz) grated suet (see page 63)
70 ml (2¹/₄ fl oz) milk

1 Prepare a 1 litre pudding basin for steaming (see Chef's techniques, page 62).

2 To make the filling, place the butter and sugars in a bowl and, using a wooden spoon or electric beaters, beat together until soft and pale. Prick the lemon all over with a thick skewer.

3 To make the suet crust, sieve together the flour and a pinch of salt into a bowl. Stir in the lemon rind and suet, then make a well in the centre and pour the milk and 60 ml (2 fl oz) water into it. Using a round-bladed knife, stir the flour into the liquid until combined into a soft dough. Lightly flour a clean surface, tip the dough onto it and knead for 5 seconds until smooth, then cut off and reserve a quarter for the lid.

4 Roll out the remaining three-quarters of the dough to a circle large enough to fill the inside of the prepared basin. Transfer the dough to the basin and ease the pastry into the rounded bowl shape, without wrinkling it, leaving a little pastry hanging over the sides.

5 Immediately place a third of the filling into the pastry-lined basin, then place the lemon centrally on top. Pack the remaining filling firmly around the lemon and fold the pastry edge over the filling. Roll out the remaining quarter of dough to the size of the top of the basin, dampen the edges and place on top of the filling to form a lid. Press together the lining dough and lid to seal well. Cover and steam for 3 hours, following the steaming method in the Chef's techniques on page 62.

6 Allow the pudding to stand for 20 minutes, then remove the string, foil and paper and turn the pudding out onto a deep serving dish to catch the 'pond' of sauce that will run out.

7 To serve, remove a portion of the crust and place on a serving plate with some of the filling. Carefully remove the lemon from the centre of the pudding and cut into four or six portions. Serve a piece with each portion of the pudding and accompany with a lemon sorbet, ice cream or cream.

Chef's tips The suet crust will continue to soak up the filling as it stands and leaving it to stand will make it easier to cut.

It is important for the lightness of the dough that the crust be made and used as quickly as possible. This will retain the bubbles being produced from the self-raising flour and liquids meeting in the mixing process.

An orange or lime could be used in place of the lemon. If using the smaller lime, the pudding could be made in four individual pudding basins, with a lime placed in each.

For a variation, flavour the crust with ground cinnamon or ginger instead of grated lemon rind, or add sultanas to the filling.

Iles flottantes

A traditional French pudding that means 'floating islands', this is an irresistible dessert of islands of soft almond meringue floating on a sea of crème anglaise.

Preparation time **30 minutes + cooling**
Total cooking time **55 minutes**
Serves 6

55 g (1³/4 oz) flaked almonds
105 g (3¹/2 oz) caster sugar
sprigs of fresh mint, to decorate

MERINGUES
4 egg whites
100 g (3¹/4 oz) caster sugar

CREME ANGLAISE
500 ml (16 fl oz) milk
1 vanilla pod, split lengthways
4 egg yolks
100 g (3¹/4 oz) caster sugar

1 Preheat a grill and toast the flaked almonds to golden brown, cool and crush lightly. Line a baking tray with greaseproof paper.

2 Prepare a caramel using the caster sugar and 105 ml (3¹/2 fl oz) water and following the method in the Chef's techniques on page 62. After the caramel has stopped cooking, immediately stir in the almonds and pour this nougatine onto the prepared tray, being careful as the tray will become very hot. Leave to cool.

3 Line the base of six 150 ml (5 fl oz) pudding moulds or ramekins with a disc of greaseproof paper. Using a palette knife or metal spatula, loosen the nougatine and lift it off the tray onto a chopping board. With a heavy sharp knife, roughly chop into 1 cm (¹/2 inch) pieces and scatter into the base of the moulds. Preheat the oven to very slow 140°C (275°F/Gas 1).

4 To make the meringues, beat the egg whites in a clean, dry bowl until soft peaks form. Add 1 tablespoon of the sugar and whisk well, then repeat until half the sugar has been added and the meringue is very stiff, smooth and satiny. Using a large metal spoon or plastic spatula, fold in the remaining half of the sugar.

5 Divide the mixture between the moulds, tap them gently on the work surface to remove air pockets, then level the tops with a palette knife. Cover each mould with a piece of lightly buttered greaseproof paper and place in a baking tin or shallow dish. Pour boiling water around them to come halfway up the moulds. Bake for about 15–20 minutes, or until a knife inserted into the centre of the meringue comes out clean.

6 To make the crème anglaise, pour the milk into a deep, heavy-based pan over medium heat. Scrape the seeds from the vanilla pod and add to the milk with the pod. Slowly bring just to the boil to allow the flavour of the vanilla to infuse into the milk. Remove from the heat. In a bowl, using a wooden spoon, cream together the yolks and the sugar until pale and thick. Pour the hot milk onto the yolks and mix well. Pour the mixture into a clean pan and cook over very gentle heat, stirring continuously, for 5 minutes, or until it begins to thicken and coats the back of a spoon. Do not allow it to boil or it will curdle. Strain the sauce into a jug and discard the vanilla pod.

7 To serve, pour the crème anglaise onto six plates. Lift the moulds out of the water bath and remove and discard the paper. If necessary, loosen the top edge of the meringues with a small knife, then turn out onto the centre of each plate and decorate with a sprig of mint. Serve warm or cold.

Banana coconut fudge pudding

A sumptuously rich pudding, where a layer of real vanilla fudge is topped with sticky banana and coconut. Serve with a spoon of thick yoghurt.

Preparation time **1 hour**
Total cooking time **1 hour 35 minutes**
Serves **6**

FUDGE
2 vanilla pods
310 g (10 oz) sugar
150 g (5 oz) unsalted butter, cut into cubes
160 ml (5¼ fl oz) thick (double) cream

60 g (2 oz) desiccated coconut
4 bananas
3 eggs
½ teaspoon vanilla extract or essence
115 g (3¾ oz) caster sugar
135 g (4½ oz) plain flour
½ teaspoon baking powder
3 tablespoons coconut cream
2½ tablespoons milk
20 g (¾ oz) unsalted butter, melted

1 Brush a 20 cm (8 inch) square or round cake tin (not one with a loose base) with melted butter. Fold a piece of greaseproof paper in half lengthways and wrap around the tin, folded-edge-downwards. Cut the paper so it is 4 cm (1½ inches) taller than the tin and the end is 2 cm (¾ inch) longer than the circumference. Snip cuts along the folded edge of the paper and place, cut-edge-down, inside the tin. Cut two pieces of baking paper to fit the base of the tin, place on the tin's base and brush with melted butter.

2 To make the fudge, prepare a caramel using the seeds from the vanilla pods, the sugar and 150 ml (5 fl oz) water, following the method in the Chef's techniques on page 62. After the caramel has stopped cooking, add the butter and reheat the caramel, stirring gently to incorporate. Remove from the heat, stir in the cream, then return the pan to the stove and bring to the boil. Pour a quarter of the fudge into the prepared tin and set aside to cool, leaving the remaining fudge in the pan for later use. Sprinkle one third of the desiccated coconut over the fudge in the tin.

3 Peel three of the bananas and cut into 5 mm (¼ inch) thick slices. Mash the remaining banana and set aside. Place the sliced bananas, slightly overlapping, on top of the fudge and coconut in the tin. Preheat the oven to warm 160°C (315°F/Gas 2–3).

4 Bring a pan half full of water to the boil, then remove from the heat. Have ready a heatproof bowl that will fit over the pan without actually touching the water. Place the eggs, vanilla and sugar in the bowl and place over the pan of steaming water. Whisk until the mixture is thick and leaves a trail across the surface when the whisk is lifted. Remove the bowl from over the water and continue whisking until cold, then sieve the flour and baking powder onto the mixture and fold in gently using a large metal spoon or plastic spatula.

5 In a large bowl, mix together the remaining desiccated coconut, the mashed banana, coconut cream, milk and melted butter, then fold gently into the mixture. Pour this mixture into the tin and bake for 1 hour 15 minutes. To test when the pudding is done, pierce with a skewer. If it comes out clean, the pudding is cooked.

6 Turn out the pudding immediately onto a serving plate. Reheat the reserved fudge and serve the pudding with the fudge and some thick yoghurt.

Tipsy cake

In Austria, where this cake originated, it is called 'Besoffener Capuziner', which can be translated as Tipsy Friar. In this version, there is enough rum for flavour, but not enough to make you tipsy!

*Preparation time **45 minutes + 30 minutes soaking + 30 minutes infusing + 4 hours soaking***
*Total cooking time **40 minutes***
Serves 6

PUDDING
55 g (1³/4 oz) raisins
2 tablespoons rum
4 eggs, separated
90 g (3 oz) caster sugar
finely grated rind of 1 orange
100 g (3¼ oz) white breadcrumbs, sieved
55 g (1³/4 oz) ground almonds
2 tablespoons milk
2 teaspoons cocoa powder

SOAKING SYRUP
150 ml (5 fl oz) water
250 g (8 oz) sugar
1 vanilla pod
1½ teaspoons coffee extract or 2 teaspoons instant coffee mixed with 1 teaspoon hot water
1½ tablespoons rum
rind of 1½ oranges
2 small cinnamon sticks
3 cloves

1 In a small bowl, soak the raisins in the rum for 30 minutes. Preheat the oven to moderate 180°C (350°F/Gas 4). Brush a 1 litre kugelhopf or ring mould with melted butter, chill to set and brush again.
2 With electric beaters, beat the egg yolks in a large bowl with half the sugar and the orange rind until pale and fluffy. Wash the whisk, dry thoroughly, and in another clean dry bowl, whisk the egg whites until stiff. Add the remaining sugar in three batches, whisking well between each addition until stiff, glossy peaks form. Using a large metal spoon or plastic spatula, fold one third of the meringue into the yolk mixture, followed by half each of the breadcrumbs, almonds and milk. Repeat, then fold in the remaining meringue. Remove one third of the mixture to a separate bowl, sift the cocoa powder into this smaller amount of cake mixture and fold in gently.
3 Drain the raisins, reserving any rum. Place half in the bottom of the tin and sprinkle the remainder onto the white cake mixture and barely fold in with two or three strokes of the spoon. Place alternate spoonfuls of the white and chocolate pudding mixtures into the tin, swirling once or twice with the handle of a spoon or spatula to get a good marbled effect. Finish with the white mixture. Bake for 30–35 minutes, or until the cake is golden brown and a skewer inserted into the centre comes out clean.
4 To make the soaking syrup, place all the ingredients in a pan with any reserved rum from the raisins and slowly bring to the boil, then remove from the stove and leave to stand and infuse for 30 minutes.
5 Loosen the edge of the cake with a palette knife and turn out onto a plate or wire rack. Replace the tin and turn over again so the cake is loose but in the tin. Strain two thirds of the syrup over the pudding, allow it to cool, then cover with plastic wrap and leave at cool room temperature for 4 hours.
6 Turn the pudding out and serve with the remaining syrup. You can fill the centre of the pudding with sweetened cream or just serve some cream on the side.

Chef's tip For a variation, use Tia Maria instead of rum.

Chocolate soufflé with crème de menthe sauce

A delicious chocolate soufflé accompanied by a light sauce of eggs, sugar and crème de menthe, which is known as 'zabaglione' to the Italians and 'sabayon' to the French.

Preparation time **25 minutes + 10 minutes cooling**
Total cooking time **1 hour**
Serves **4–6**

60 g (2 oz) good-quality dark chocolate, preferably
   bitter, roughly chopped
125 ml (4 fl oz) milk
2 tablespoons cocoa powder
2 tablespoons plain flour, sieved
30 g (1 oz) caster sugar
1/4 teaspoon vanilla extract or essence
3 egg yolks
4 egg whites
cocoa powder, to dust
chocolate curls, to decorate, optional

CREME DE MENTHE SAUCE
1 egg
3 egg yolks
2 1/2 tablespoons caster sugar
1 1/2 tablespoons white crème de menthe

1 Brush a 1.5 litre charlotte tin with some melted butter, dust it with caster sugar, then lightly tap and empty out any excess sugar. Half fill the pan that will sit beneath your steamer with water and slowly bring to the boil.

2 Place the chocolate in a bowl and pour the milk into a small pan. Bring the milk to the boil, then pour onto the chocolate and stir with a wooden spoon until the chocolate is melted and the mixture smooth. Return the mixture to the pan with the cocoa and bring just to the boil. Add the flour and quickly beat together with a wooden spoon over low heat for 2 minutes, or until the mixture is smooth and rolls away readily from the bottom and side of the pan. Remove from the stove, stir in the sugar and vanilla and cool for about 10 minutes, or until lukewarm. Add the yolks one at a time, beating the mixture well between each addition.

3 Put the egg whites into a clean dry bowl and whisk with a balloon whisk or electric beaters until stiff peaks form. Using a large metal spoon or plastic spatula, briskly fold 1 tablespoon of egg white into the chocolate mixture to soften it, then carefully fold in the remaining egg white.

4 Immediately pour the mixture into the prepared tin and cover with plastic wrap. Place it in the steamer over the boiling water. Turn the heat down to a gentle simmer, cover the steamer with a lid 'almost on' or a piece of foil pierced with a few holes. Steam with the water gently bubbling for about 40–45 minutes, or until well risen and firm to the touch. Remove the tin from the steamer and set aside while making the sauce.

5 To make the crème de menthe sauce, place all the ingredients in a heatproof bowl that can sit over the water in the steamer pan. Lightly whisk the ingredients together, then place the bowl over the steaming water and continue to whisk until the mixture is light and frothy and when the whisk is lifted just above the surface, the sauce falls back to leave a ribbon-like trail.

6 To serve, remove the plastic wrap from the soufflé and turn out onto a plate. Dust with cocoa and decorate with chocolate curls. Serve immediately with the sauce.

Chef's tips The soufflé will turn out easily if left to stand for 5 minutes. Do not leave it in the steamer or it will overcook in its own residual heat.

Do not make the sauce in advance because it may separate and become liquid at the bottom if left to stand.

Eton mess

Named after the famous school, this easy pudding is perfect for summer's abundance of strawberries. A great way to use up overripe fruit and leftover or broken meringues.

Preparation time **25 minutes + 4 hours marinating**
Total cooking time **Nil**
Serves 4

600 g (1 1/4 lb) strawberries, hulled
4 tablespoons Grand Marnier
1 vanilla pod, split lengthways
45 g (1 1/2 oz) caster sugar
30 g (1 oz) ready-made meringues
400 ml (12 3/4 fl oz) thick (double) or cream,
   for whipping

1 Set aside four good strawberries for decoration. Place the remaining strawberries in a large bowl and roughly crush with a fork. Add the Grand Marnier, vanilla pod and sugar, cover with plastic wrap and marinate in the refrigerator for at least 4 hours. Remove and discard the vanilla pod, then spoon one third of the mixture into four wine glasses. Break the meringues roughly into about 1.5 cm (5/8 inch) pieces.

2 Pour the cream into a bowl and, using a balloon whisk or electric beaters, whip the cream until just thick, but so that it still runs if the bowl is tipped.

3 Add the cream to the remaining two thirds of the strawberry mixture and, using a large metal spoon or plastic spatula, fold together until streaky and half combined. Add two thirds of the broken meringue and continue to fold until evenly combined.

4 Spoon the meringue mixture onto the crushed strawberries in the wine glasses. Crush the remaining meringue a little more and sprinkle it over the surface, then decorate with a whole strawberry.

Plum charlotte

Usually made with apple, this plum charlotte is a delicious variation on a classic. Careful lining of the mould will ensure that the pudding turns out beautifully.

Preparation time 35 minutes + 1 hour cooling
Total cooking time 55 minutes

Serves 6

17 thin slices of white bread, trimmed of crusts
250 g (8 oz) unsalted butter
105 g (3¹/₂ oz) white breadcrumbs
90 g (3 oz) soft light brown sugar
1 kg (2 lb) red plums, fresh or canned, stoned
   and cut into 1.5 cm (⁵/₈ inch) pieces
a little lemon rind
pinch of ground cinnamon
75 g (2¹/₂ oz) apricot jam

1 Brush a 2 litre charlotte mould or soufflé dish with a little melted butter. Cut six slices of bread in half to form rectangles and cut seven slices in half at a diagonal to form triangles. Reserve the remaining four slices.

2 Turn the mould upside down and place the bread triangles on top, overlapping the edges to completely cover the top of the mould. Hold the triangles in place and, using the mould as a guide, trim the excess edges with scissors so the triangles will fit inside the base of the mould exactly. Reserve the trimmings.

3 Melt 200 g (6¹/₂ oz) of the butter in a pan, dip the bread triangles in, then line the base of the mould, butter-side-down. Dip the rectangles in the butter and arrange around the sides, butter-side-out, overlapping the edges until the mould is completely covered and filling any gaps with the bread trimmings. Dip the reserved slices of bread in the butter and set aside.

4 To make the filling, melt half the remaining butter in a large pan, add the breadcrumbs and cook, stirring, until golden brown. Drain on crumpled paper towels. In another pan, gently heat the remaining butter and the brown sugar, stir well to dissolve, then cook without stirring until light caramel in colour. Add the plums and gently cook, stirring frequently, until just starting to soften (if you are using canned plums, you will only need to heat them through). Remove from the stove, add the lemon rind, cinnamon and breadcrumbs and stir gently to combine.

5 Preheat the oven to moderately hot 190°C (375°F/ Gas 5). Ladle the filling into the prepared mould until half full. Cover with half the reserved bread slices, press down firmly to level, then add the remaining filling. If the filling is not level with the mould lining, trim the bread with a small knife or scissors. Cover with the remaining bread pieces, butter-side-up, taking care to fill any gaps. Press in gently and cover with foil.

6 Place the charlotte on a baking tray and bake for about 40 minutes, or until golden and firm. Leave for about 1 hour to cool completely before turning out onto a serving plate.

7 In a small pan, heat the apricot jam with about 1¹/₂ tablespoons water. When the mixture has melted and begins to boil, sieve it into a small bowl and, while still hot, brush it over the surface of the charlotte.

Chef's tip Some varieties of plums have thicker skins than others. If you wish to remove the skins, dip the plums in boiling water for 10–20 seconds, quickly cool in iced water, then skin before stoning them.

Steamed orange pudding

Hot, light and full of flavour, this pudding will brighten the gloom of a winter's day like a burst of summer sunshine. Serve with the orange sauce or custard.

*Preparation time **30 minutes***
*Total cooking time **1 hour 45 minutes***
Serves 6

100 g (3¼ oz) thin-cut marmalade
2 large oranges, peel and pith removed
125 g (4 oz) unsalted butter, at room temperature
125 g (4 oz) caster sugar
finely grated rind of 1 orange
2 large eggs, beaten
185 g (6 oz) self-raising flour
milk, for mixing

ORANGE SAUCE
320 ml (10½ fl oz) orange juice
2 egg yolks
½ teaspoon cornflour
45 g (1½ oz) caster sugar
1 teaspoon Grand Marnier or Cointreau

1 Prepare a 1.25 litre pudding basin for steaming (see Chef's techniques, page 62).

2 Spoon the marmalade into the pudding basin. Finely slice the oranges, then line the basin with the orange slices, from the marmalade base to the top of the bowl.

3 In a bowl, beat the butter with a wooden spoon or electric whisk to soften. Slowly add the sugar, beating until light and creamy. Mix in the orange rind. Add the egg in six additions, beating well between each addition. Sieve in the flour and quickly fold into the mixture using a large metal spoon or plastic spatula. As the last traces of flour are mixed in, add a little milk to form a soft consistency: the mixture should drop from the spoon with a flick of the wrist.

4 Immediately spoon the mixture into the prepared pudding basin, cover and steam for 1½–1¾ hours, following the steaming method in the Chef's techniques on page 62. To test when the pudding is done, pierce with a skewer. If it comes out clean, the pudding is cooked.

5 Remove the string, foil and paper and turn the pudding out onto a serving plate (if you are not serving the pudding immediately, place the bowl back over the pudding to prevent it drying out).

6 To make the orange sauce, bring the orange juice to the boil in a small pan. In a bowl, beat the egg yolks, cornflour and sugar until thick and light. Pour the hot orange juice into the bowl, mix until blended, then return to the pan. Cook over medium heat, stirring constantly with a wooden spoon, until the mixture coats the back of the spoon and the sauce does not close over when a line is drawn across the spoon with a finger.

7 Remove from the heat, strain into a bowl, then stir in the Grand Marnier or Cointreau. If you are not using the sauce straight away, dust the surface lightly with caster sugar to prevent a skin forming. The sugar can be stirred in just before serving. Serve the sauce warm or cold with the pudding.

Lemon delicious

Also known as 'Lemon surprise' or just 'Lemon pudding', this wonderful pudding separates as it cooks into a light soufflé sponge topping with a tart lemon sauce hidden beneath.

Preparation time **25 minutes**
Total cooking time **40 minutes**
Serves 4

60 g (2 oz) unsalted butter, at room temperature
95 g (3 1/4 oz) caster sugar
finely grated rind of 1 lemon
2 large eggs, separated
2 tablespoons plain flour
3 tablespoons lemon juice
250 ml (8 fl oz) milk
icing sugar, for dusting

1 Preheat the oven to moderate 180°C (350°F/Gas 4). Brush a 20.5 x 15 x 4.5 cm (8 1/4 x 6 x 1 3/4 inch) ovenproof dish with butter.

2 Using a wooden spoon or electric beaters, beat the butter to soften it, then beat in the sugar in small additions. Continue beating until the mixture is light and creamy, then mix in the lemon rind and egg yolks until well blended. Gently fold in the flour, followed by the lemon juice.

3 In a small pan, warm the milk until tepid, then fold it into the lemon mixture.

4 Place the egg whites in a large clean dry bowl, add a pinch of salt and beat them with a balloon whisk or electric beaters until soft peaks form. Using a plastic spatula or a large metal spoon, mix 1 tablespoon of the egg white into the lemon mixture to soften it, then carefully fold in the remaining egg white, being careful not to lose volume.

5 Pour the mixture into the prepared dish, then stand in a baking tray or shallow ovenproof dish and pour warm water around to come about two thirds up the sides. Bake for 30–35 minutes, or until the top is a pale golden brown and firm to the light touch of a finger. Serve the pudding hot or chilled. If you are serving it cold, dust with a little sifted icing sugar before serving.

Chef's tip When the lemon juice meets the butter, the mixture may curdle. However, when you add the milk, the mixture should become smooth again (make sure the milk is barely warm—if it is too hot, the flour and yolks will cook at this stage and the pudding may become too heavy).

Traditional rice pudding

This classic favourite, so simple to prepare, cooks slowly and gently in the oven, allowing the rice time to absorb all the liquid. The result is delightfully soft and creamy.

Preparation time **5 minutes + 30 minutes standing**
Total cooking time **2 hours**
Serves 4

750 ml (24 fl oz) milk
20 g (3/4 oz) caster sugar
2–3 drops vanilla extract or essence
75 g (2¹/2 oz) short-grain rice
unsalted butter, for topping
freshly grated nutmeg, to taste

1 Combine the milk, sugar, vanilla and rice in a 1 litre pie or ovenproof dish and leave to stand for 30 minutes. Preheat the oven to moderate 180°C (350°F/Gas 4).
2 Dot the butter over the mixture, sprinkle some nutmeg over the top and cover with foil. Place the dish on the middle shelf of the oven and bake for 1 hour, stirring once or twice with a fork.
3 Remove the foil and reduce the oven temperature to slow 150°C (300°F/Gas 2). If serving the pudding cold, bake for another 45 minutes, leave to cool, then refrigerate until ready to serve. If serving hot, cook for 1 hour, or until a brown skin forms and the interior of the pudding is soft and creamy. Serve hot with a teaspoon of strawberry jam or cold with red berries or poached red plums.

Chef's tips If the rice pudding is too dry, adjust the consistency before serving by lifting the skin to one side and adding a little cold milk.

To vary the flavour, use cinnamon in place of the vanilla and nutmeg, or sprinkle some sultanas or chopped mixed peel in with the rice before cooking.

Chocolate fondant soufflés

The 'fondant' aspect of these simple but devastatingly effective chocolate fixes is the hot centre, which spills slowly across the plate when the crisp shell of the soufflé is broken open.

Preparation time **35 minutes + 5 minutes cooling**
Total cooking time **20 minutes**
Serves 6

120 g (4 oz) dark bitter chocolate, chopped
120 g (4 oz) unsalted butter, at room temperature
2 eggs
2 egg yolks
90 g (3 oz) caster sugar
2 teaspoons cocoa powder
60 g (2 oz) plain bread flour
3/4 teaspoon baking powder
cocoa powder, for dusting

1 Thickly brush six 150 ml (5 fl oz) ramekins with some melted butter, dust with caster sugar, then lightly tap and empty out any excess sugar. Preheat the oven to moderate 180°C (350°F/Gas 4).

2 Bring a pan half full of water to the boil, then remove from the heat. Have ready a heatproof bowl that will fit over the pan without actually touching the water. Put the chocolate and butter in the bowl and place over the pan of steaming water. Leave to stand until the chocolate has melted, then stir with a wooden spoon until the butter is incorporated and the mixture is smooth and glossy. Remove the bowl from over the pan of steaming water and allow to cool for 5 minutes.

3 Place the whole eggs, yolks and sugar in another bowl and whisk until pale and thick. Fold into the chocolate mixture using a large metal spoon (the mixture should not be totally incorporated at this stage).

4 Sieve the cocoa powder, flour and baking powder onto the mixture and, using a large metal spoon or plastic spatula, fold in gently until no pale streaks are visible. Pour the mixture into the prepared ramekins and bake for 15–18 minutes.

5 When the puddings are cooked, allow to stand for 2 minutes, then turn out and dust with cocoa powder. Serve immediately with raspberries and cream.

Chef's tip The molten centre of these soufflés is dependent on a very precise cooking time. Since all ovens vary slightly in temperature, if you are making these for a special occasion, you may wish to do a practise run first.

Chef's techniques

◆

Steaming puddings

Make sure your pudding basin will fit in your pan with the lid on.

Thickly brush a pudding basin with melted butter. Line the base of the pudding basin with a disc of greaseproof paper.

Lay a sheet of foil on the work surface and cover with a sheet of greaseproof paper. Make a large pleat in the middle and grease the paper with some melted butter.

Place the mixture in the basin and hollow the surface slightly with the back of a wet spoon. Place the foil, paper-side-down, across the top and tie string securely around the rim and over the top to make a handle.

Place a saucer or trivet in a large pan and rest the pudding basin on it. Half-fill the pan with boiling water and bring to the boil. Cover and simmer until cooked, topping up the water if needed with more boiling water.

Making caramel

Using water to dissolve your sugar in gives a greater degree of control for caramel-making.

Place the caster sugar and water in a heavy-based pan. Fill a shallow pan with cold water and set it next to the stove.

Stir over low heat to dissolve the sugar. To prevent sugar crystals from forming, brush down the sides of the pan with a brush dipped in water.

Bring to the boil and simmer until the caramel takes on a deep golden colour. Swirl the pan to stop the caramel colouring unevenly.

Stop the cooking by plunging the bottom of the pan into the cold water for a few seconds.

Making crêpes

A crêpe pan makes crêpe-making much easier, especially if you keep it just for this.

Over medium heat, melt some clarified butter or oil in a 15–17 cm (6–7 inch) heavy-based or non-stick pan. When a haze forms, pour out any excess butter.

Stir the batter well and pour into the pan from a ladle or jug, starting in the centre and swirling the pan to create a thin coating. Tip out any excess.

Cook for 1 minute until bubbles appear, the batter sets and the edges are brown. Carefully loosen and lift the edges with a palette knife. Turn and cook for 30 seconds until golden. Remove from the pan and repeat.

Grating suet

If ready-prepared suet is not available, make your own by grating fresh suet.

Prepare the suet by grating it by hand or by using a food processor.

Making baba dough

Using your hand to beat baba dough is more effective than a spoon.

Using the fingers of one hand, held lightly apart, bring the ingredients together to form a soft elastic dough. Beat with the hand for about 5 minutes, or until smooth.

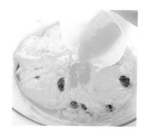

Add the raisins and rum and beat with your hand to combine. Scrape down the sides of the bowl and pour the warm butter over the surface of the dough.

Cover and leave to prove for about 30 minutes, or until doubled in volume. Beat the baba mixture to incorporate the butter.

Spoon the mixture into a piping bag fitted with a 2 cm (3/4 inch) plain nozzle and pipe into the tins. Cover with a damp cloth and prove until the mixture reaches the tops of the tins.

Published in 1999 by Merehurst Limited, Ferry House, 51–57 Lacy Road, Putney, London SW15 1PR.

Merehurst Limited, Murdoch Books and Le Cordon Bleu thank the 32 masterchefs of all the Le Cordon Bleu Schools, whose knowledge and expertise have made this book possible, especially: Chef Terrien, Chef Boucheret, Chef Duchêne (MOF), Chef Guillut, Chef Pinaud, Paris; Chef Males, Chef Walsh, Chef Power, Chef Neveu, Chef Paton, Chef Poole-Gleed, Chef Wavrin, London; Chef Chantefort, Chef Nicaud, Chef Jambert, Chef Honda, Tokyo; Chef Salambien, Chef Boutin, Chef Harris, Sydney; Chef Lawes, Adelaide; Chef Guiet, Chef Denis, Chef Petibon, Chef Jean Michel Poncet, Ottawa. Of the many students who helped the Chefs test each recipe, a special mention to graduates Hollace Hamilton and Alice Buckley. A very special acknowledgment to Helen Barnard, Alison Oakervee and Deepika Sukhwani, who have been responsible for the coordination of the Le Cordon Bleu team throughout this series under the Presidency of André Cointreau.

Series Manager: Kay Halsey
Series Concept, Design and Art Direction: Juliet Cohen
Food Editor: Lulu Grimes
Designer: Norman Baptista
Photographers: Jon Bader, Craig Cranko
Food Stylists: Kay Francis, Mary Harris
Food Preparation: Michelle Earl, Kerrie Mullins
Chef's Techniques Photographer: Reg Morrison
Home Economists: Michelle Earl, Michelle Lawton, Michaela Le Compte, Maria Villegas

Creative Director: Marylouise Brammer
International Sales Director: Mark Newman
CEO & Publisher: Anne Wilson

ISBN 1 85391 789 3

Printed by Toppan Printing Hong Kong Co. Ltd. PRINTED IN CHINA
First Printed 1999
©Design and photography Murdoch Books® 1999
©Text Le Cordon Bleu 1999

A catalogue record for this book is available from the British Library.

Distributed in the UK by D Services, 6 Euston Street, Freemen's Common, Leicester LE2 7SS Tel 0116-254-7671 Fax 0116-254-4670.
Distributed in Canada by Whitecap (Vancouver) Ltd, 351 Lynn Avenue, North Vancouver, BC V7J 2C4 Tel 604-980-9852 Fax 604-980-8197 or Whitecap (Ontario) Ltd, 47 Coldwater Road, North York, ON M3B 1Y8 Tel 416-444-3442 Fax 416-444-6630
Published and distributed in Australia by Murdoch Books®, GPO Box 1203, Sydney NSW 1045

The Publisher and Le Cordon Bleu wish to thank Hale Enterprises Pty Ltd., Hale Imports Pty Ltd. and Villeroy & Boch Australia Pty Ltd. for their assistance in the photography
Front cover: Layered blackcurrant pudding (back), Treacle pudding (middle) and Ginger pudding with kumquat and ginger compote

---

IMPORTANT INFORMATION

CONVERSION GUIDE

1 cup = 250 ml (8 fl oz)
1 Australian tablespoon = 20 ml (4 teaspoons)
1 UK tablespoon = 15 ml (3 teaspoons)

NOTE: We have used 20 ml tablespoons. If you are using a 15 ml tablespoon, for most recipes the difference will be negligible. For recipes using baking powder, gelatine, bicarbonate of soda and flour, add an extra teaspoon for each tablespoon specified.

CUP CONVERSIONS—DRY INGREDIENTS

1 cup flour, plain or self-raising = 125 g (4 oz)
1 cup sugar, caster = 250 g (8 oz)
1 cup breadcrumbs, dry = 125 g (4 oz)

IMPORTANT: Those who might be at risk from the effects of salmonella food poisoning (the elderly, pregnant women, young children and those suffering from immune deficiency diseases) should consult their GP with any concerns about eating raw eggs.